The Sa...

SYD...

SMITH

edited by

ALAN BELL

Duckworth

First published in 1993 by
Gerald Duckworth & Co. Ltd.
The Old Piano Factory
48 Hoxton Square, London N1 6PB
Tel: 071 729 5986
Fax: 071 729 0015

Introduction and editorial arrangement
© 1993 by Gerald Duckworth & Co. Ltd.

All rights reserved. No part of this publication
may be reproduced, stored in a retrieval system, or
transmitted, in any form or by any means, electronic,
mechanical, photocopying, recording or otherwise,
without the prior permission of the publisher.

A catalogue record for this book is available
from the British Library

ISBN 0 7156 2391 5

Typeset by Ray Davies
Printed in Great Britain by
Redwood Press Limited, Melksham

Contents

6 Introduction

11 Autobiographical

17 Scotland & the Scotch

20 The Edinburgh Review

22 Literature

25 Wit & Humour

27 Gastronomica

32 Friends & Contemporaries

36 Town & Country

38 Church & Clergy

46 Politics

53 Toleration & Intolerance

56 Law & Punishment

58 Education

60 Women & Marriage

62 Counsels & Maxims

Introduction

Sydney Smith's fame as a conversational wit ensured that many of his sayings were preserved by London society in the first half of the nineteenth century, just as the sprightliness of his correspondence meant that many of his letters were treasured by their recipients. This enables an anthologist in the *Sayings of* … series to include a satisfying proportion of well-attested *dicta* as well as a selection of more considered literary apophthegms. Smith's table-talk, fast in repartee, full of casual puns and flights of fancy, and with an unmalicious edge, cannot be recalled except in its general style. It is clear however that the plums noted by hilariously amused contemporaries were part of an infectious flow of conversational humour. Equally, his letters and published writings confirm his reputation for wisdom as well as for wit. There is good sense and sound advice to be found there in profusion; never heavily sententious, he was usually capable of being serious without being solemn.

Born on 3rd June 1771, the second of four sons of a prosperous but unsympathetic father with business interests in the India trade, Sydney Smith was educated at Winchester (which he disliked) and at New College, Oxford (which he was soon to criticise for the narrowness of the university curriculum). A New College fellowship led to his being ordained, though he had not intended a career as a clergyman; his progress in the Church was indeed to be painfully slow. His first curacy, in a parish on Salisbury Plain, led to a friendship with the local squire, Mr Hicks Beach and his wife, and he became tutor to their sons, accompanying them to study in Edinburgh when the war made continental travel impossible.

It was in Edinburgh that he first flourished, falling in with a lively set of bright young Whig advocates opposed to the prevailing Tory domination of the country. With Francis Jeffrey (later Lord Advocate and a

Scots judge) as editor, and Henry Brougham (later Lord Chancellor), among others, Smith was a projector of the *Edinburgh Review*, the liberal literary and political quarterly first published in 1801. He was connected with it for nearly thirty years, with many anonymous, but identifiable, review-articles to his credit. His subjects included the civil disabilities of Roman Catholics, the harsh Game Laws of the time, the transportation of felons and other aspects of penal policy, university reform, and some mockery of the extremes of Dissenting enthusiasm. The *Review* had a success and influence far beyond its projectors' expectations, and was much imitated by other political groups, setting a pattern for British periodical journalism throughout the century.

In 1803, Sydney Smith, who had married and started a family while in Edinburgh, moved to London, supporting himself with literary and occasional preaching work. He also held a temporary lectureship at the Royal Institution, where a highly successful course of subscription lectures (published much later as *Elementary Sketches of Moral Philosophy*) greatly increased his social reputation. His political campaigning for the Roman Catholics (he had no sympathy for their religious beliefs) continued, and in 1807 came *Letters on the Subject of the Catholics*, condemning the average Protestant's attitude to the civil restrictions imposed on Catholics by out-of-date laws. These sprightly pamphlets, written by one 'Peter Plymley' to his dim country-parson brother Abraham, achieved a wide circulation. Though pseudonymous, the authorship of the *Plymley Letters* was widely known among Sydney Smith's circle, and increased his standing in the prominent Whig salon kept by Lord and Lady Holland at Holland House in Kensington.

Shortly before the *Letters* started to appear, Sydney Smith had been appointed to a northern parish lying between York and Malton. He was initially allowed not to reside there; a York curate ran the parish for him. Before long, however, he found himself obliged by the ecclesiastical authorities to take charge of the parish himself. Reluctant though he was to leave London, and much though he joked about the longueurs of country living, he accepted the challenge of Yorkshire exile with reasonably good grace. He moved to Foston, 'twelve miles from a lemon', not in a spirit of mere resignation but with the intention of becoming an active country parson. His record of parochial work is a good one, including the setting up of a dispensary and a savings bank as extensions of his ministry. Remote though his parish seemed from London, it was near enough to the Edinburgh road to guarantee a stream of visitors to the bright rectory he built there for his growing family, and there were agreeable neighbours – especially Lord Carlisle and his family at Castle Howard – to alleviate the rural round. He continued to write for the *Edinburgh Review* and kept up his correspondence with London and Edinburgh friends.

He was active locally in campaigns for Catholic Emancipation and Parliamentary Reform, and as the political tide gradually turned in favour of his Whig associates he was rewarded by some promotion in the Church. First came a canonry at Bristol (1828-31), then in its place a more lucrative stall at St Paul's Cathedral, to which he was appointed in 1831. The Yorkshire parish was also exchanged for the living of Combe Florey, near Taunton, and his St Paul's appointment enabled him to move to London for cathedral duties but to retain the Somerset parish.

In the 1830s and until his death in 1845 Sydney Smith confirmed his metropolitan reputation as a diner-out, and many of his recorded sayings belong to this period. In London he found himself well endowed with the appreciative audience whose applause he had long before seen as essential to the dramatic requirements of a witty man. His lectures had seen the '*mere* wit', one with an appetite only for the amusing and not for the useful relations of ideas, as being a character of limited worth. His own aim and achievement had gone deeper than an aspiration to be known as a sayer of good things. The oral record, of actual sayings, is full and creditable. His writings, however, amplify with plentiful examples of verbal wit the often rather flattening contemporary record of his talk.

In later publications, such as the *Letters to Archdeacon Singleton* in which he attacked the policies of the Ecclesiastical Commissioners (but incidentally showed the limits of his zeal for reform), are as spirited as Peter Plymley and his *Edinburgh Review* articles. And perhaps above all it is in his letters that we can appreciate the verve and banter, and the lightness of touch, which combined with the common sense of his published writings to endear him to his contemporaries.

He failed to achieve the reward of a bishopric, though he himself had always been sceptical of his chances of achieving a mitre. His promotion to the episcopal bench was from time to time discussed among his political friends, but he may with some justice have been reckoned to be lacking in safeness and seriousness. George III is said to have remarked, around 1809, that 'he was a very clever fellow, but he would never be a bishop'. So it was to be: but Sydney felt no deprivation in avoiding the pomp of the lawn-sleeved episcopate. His canonry at St Paul's, combined with his much-loved Somerset living, sufficed.

Like many buoyantly humorous men, he was privately not immune from moments of depression, and he was able to give 'advice on low spirits' all the more convincingly from his personal experience. In his later years he was much afflicted by gout, which restricted his appetite and diminished his social personality; London acquaintances were sometimes disappointed by his failure to come up to expectation. Stout and jovial, with a rather weak mouth but a keen and kindly eye, he enjoyed generally good health until he found himself 'disglued and unscrewed' by an old age made less ungrateful by a belated access of wealth. He died at his house in Green Street, Mayfair, on 22nd February 1845, in his seventy-fourth year.

Sources

Smith's *Works* were first published in 1839/40 and there are many nineteenth-century reprints. They include most of his *Edinburgh Review* contributions. The pseudonymous *Letters of Peter Plymley* (1807-8) and the signed *Letters to Archdeacon Singleton* (1837-40) are also included, with some later sermons and miscellaneous writings. There is a posthumous edition (1850) of *Elementary Sketches of Moral Philosophy*, his Royal Institution lectures of 1804-6.

His daughter Saba, Lady Holland, published a *Memoir* of her father, with a selection from his letters (2 vols, 1855). The *Memoir* is a major source of recorded sayings, and there are well-attested anecdotes in many biographies of his contemporaries, particularly Richard Monckton Milnes, Lord Houghton, who gathered many in his notebooks. Nowell C. Smith's two-volume edition of the *Letters* (OUP, 1952) is standard but far from complete, and there is a *Selected Letters* (OUP, 1956, and reprinted 1980). A complete revision remains in preparation, but much new material has been drawn on in Alan Bell's *Sydney Smith* (OUP, 1980), the standard modern biography. These sources are all cited briefly in this anthology, for which minor adjustments of spelling and punctuation have been made in the interests of simple presentation of the text.

Autobiographical

The Smiths never had any arms, and have invariably sealed their letters with their thumbs.

Memoir

My brother [Bobus] and I have inverted the laws of nature. He rose by his gravity; I sank by my levity.

I was at school and college with the Archbishop of Canterbury [Howley]: fifty-three years ago he knocked me down with the chess-board for checkmating him – and now he is attempting to take away my patronage. I believe these are the only two acts of violence he ever committed in his life.

Singleton Letters, I

Squire: 'If I had a son who was an idiot, by Jove, I'd make him a parson.'
Smith: 'Very probably, but I see that your father was of a different mind.'

I attend the hospitals where I learn the elements of a puke and the rudiments of purging. The viscera rustica will pay for this when I am settled in my parish.

Letter, 1799

I continue to preach every now and then, and see the faithful yawning at my feet – but however if they will gape and swallow, I will forgive them one for the sake of the other.

Letter, 1799

Every parson and every relation of the said parson imagine that the moment he is connected with a Lord, that he has nothing to do but study Tithe Law, to amuse himself in planning barns of different constructions, and to order a buggy of the very best sacerdotal shape. As for me, I confess my ideas are rather lower and more practical: a few dinners, my salary well paid, the power of applying for a frank, a bow in the public streets, and a good deal of commendation behind my back. These are the limits of my expectations, and the probable limits of my good fortune.   Letter, 1801

Two or three random sermons I have discharged [in London], and thought I perceived that the greater part of the congregation thought me mad. The clerk was as pale as death in helping me off with my gown, for fear I should bite him.   *Memoir*

Je suis curé, et je le serai toujours; but as there must be hewers of wood and drawers of water in every community, so also in the Church there must be makers of sermons and baptizers, and buriers of the dead. The sweet privilege of doing nothing cannot be enjoyed at all.   Letter, 1805

If you do make me a Bishop I shall never do you discredit; for I believe that it is out of the power of lawn and velvet, and the crisp hair of dead men fashioned into a wig, to make me a dishonest man.

Letter, 1808

When I began to thump the cushion of my pulpit, on first coming to Foston, as is my wont when I preach, the accumulated dust of a hundred and fifty years made such a cloud, that for some minutes I lost sight of my congregation.   *Memoir*

My living in Yorkshire was so far out of the way that it was actually twelve miles from a lemon.   *Memoir*

In short, if it be my lot to crawl, I will crawl contentedly; if to fly, I will fly with alacrity; but as long as I can possibly avoid it I will never be unhappy.   Letter, 1809

We now have another bed, in which a maid or a philosopher, or a maid with a philosopher, might be put. God grant in this latter event that they might both merit their respective appellations the ensuing morning.
                                                            Letter, 1810

I suspect [my pamphlets] are long since hurried away to the confectioner. The season for hot tarts is over, and few pamphlets have escaped.   Letter, 1812

Lady Caroline stabbed herself at Lady Ilchester's ball for the love of Lord Byron. What a charming thing to be a Poet. I preached for many years in London and was rather popular, but never heard of a Lady doing herself the smallest mischief on my account.   Letter, 1813

I am writing to you at two o'clock in the morning, having heard of a clergyman who brought himself down from twenty-six to sixteen stone in six months, by lessening his sleep. I shall be so thin when you see me, that you may trundle me about like a mop.
                                                            Letter, 1818

I love liberty, but hope that it can be so managed that I shall have soft beds, good dinners, fine linen, etc, for the rest of my life.   Letter, 1830

There are substances in nature called amalgams, whose property is to combine incongruous materials; now I am a moral amalgam, and have a peculiar talent for mixing up human materials in society, however repellent their natures.   *Memoir*

My constitutional gaiety comes to my aid in all the difficulties of life; and the recollection that, having embraced the character of an honest man and a friend to rational liberty, I have no business to repine at that mediocrity of fortune which I *knew* to be its consequence.
                                                              Letter, 1820

When my merits are properly understood and rewarded in the Church, I will subscribe to the Athenaeum or any other club you please; but I have not risen at present (nor shall I ever rise) beyond mutton chops and the Gray's Inn coffee house.   Letter, 1924

Your Unitarian preachers have stolen away four of my Congregation who have withstood Ranters and Methodists. I shall make reprisals and open a Chapel near the College – but it shall be a generous and polite warfare, such as is the duty and not the disgrace of Christian divines.   Letter, 1826

I have taken possession of my preferment [at St Paul's]. The house is in Amen-corner – an awkward name on a card, and an awkward annunciation to the coachman on leaving any fashionable mansion.   Letter, 1831

I am not yet by a great deal clear of my fit of the gout. It has made a long stay for so recent an acquaintance.
                                                              Letter, 1834

I can't accept your invitation, for my house is full of country cousins. I wish they were once removed.
Letter, 1836

One evil in old age is that as your time is come you think every little illness is the beginning of the end. When a man expects to be arrested every knock at the door is an alarm. Letter, 1836

I was measured for a cork jacket yesterday. Walking is out of the question just now. We can only get from place to place by swimming. Letter, December 1838

There is a New Zealand attorney just arrived in London, with 6*s*.8*d*. tattooed all over his face. *Memoir*

This [1840] is the only sensible spring I remember. It is the real March of intellect. *Memoir*

I quite agree with you as to the horrors of correspondence. Correspondences are like small-clothes before the invention of suspenders: it is impossible to keep them up. Letter, 1841

I had last week an attack of the gout, which is receding from me (as a bailiff from the house of an half-pay captain) dissatisfied and terrified of the powers of colchicum. Letter, 1842

When I have the gout, I feel as if I was walking on my eyeballs.

[Rogers] had candles placed all round the dining room, in order to show off the pictures. 'I asked Smith how he liked the plan.' 'Not at all,' he replied, 'above, there is a blaze of light, and below, nothing but darkness and gnashing of teeth.'   *Rogers's Table Talk*

It would-be rather out of etiquette for a Canon of St Paul's to-go to an opera; and where etiquette prevents me from doing things disagreeable to myself, I am a perfect martinet.   Letter, 1842

I am engaged to dine with Mrs Sartoris the singing woman. Not that I have any pleasure in the voice of singing men or singing women – but as Adam said when they found him in breeches, 'The woman asked me and I did eat.'

Letter, 1843

Poverty is no disgrace to a man, but it is confoundedly inconvenient.

I shall benefit [from my brother's estate] to the amount of about £30,000 or more, which will come just in time to gild the nails of my coffin.   Letter, 1843

The whole of my life has been passed like a razor in hot water or a scrape.

I am not fond of expecting catastrophes, but there are cracks in the universe.

Praise is the best diet for us, after all.   *Memoir*

Scotland & the Scotch

That knuckle-end of England, that land of oatcakes and sulphur.

Memoir

It requires a surgical operation to get a joke well into a Scotch understanding. Their only idea of wit, or rather that inferior variety of the electric talent which prevails occasionally in the North, and which, under the name of WUT, is so infinitely distressing to people of good taste, is laughing immoderately at stated intervals.

Memoir

[The Scotch] are so imbued with metaphysics that they even make love metaphysically. I overheard a young lady of my acquaintance, at a dance in Edinburgh, exclaim, in a sudden pause in the music, 'What you say, my Lord, is very true of love in the *aibstract*, but ...' here the fiddlers began fiddling furiously, and the rest was lost.

Memoir

No smells were ever equal to Scotch smells. It is the School of Physic; walk the streets, and you would imagine that every medical man had been administering cathartics to every man, woman and child in the town. Yet the place [Edinburgh] is uncommonly beautiful, and I am in a constant balance between admiration and trepidation: Taste guides my eye, where e'er new beauties spread. While prudence whispers, 'Look before you tread.'

Letter, 1798

Now what I object to Scotch philosophers in general is
that they reason upon man as they would reason upon
X; they pursue truth without caring if it be useful truth.
They are more fond of disputing upon mind and matter
than on anything which can have a reference to the real
world inhabited by real men, women and children. In
short, a Scotchman is apt to be a practical rogue upon
sale, or a visionary philosopher.

Letter, 1801

We will pass many evenings together [at Edinburgh],
arguing and joking amidst eating and drinking – above
all being stupid when we feel inclined, a rare privilege
of friendship of which I am frequently glad to avail
myself.

Letter, 1801

I take the liberty to send you two brace of grouse –
curious, because killed by a Scotch metaphysician. In
other and better language, they are mere ideas, shot by
other ideas, out of a pure intellectual notion called a gun.

Letter, 1808

It is customary to fumigate Scotch tutors. They are
excellent men but require this little preliminary caution.

Letter, 1809

Lord Holland is quite right to get a stock of eatable
sheep, but such sheep are not exclusively the product of
Scotland, but of every half-starved, ill-cultivated
country; and are only emphatically termed *Scotch*, to
signify *ill-fed*, as one says *Roman*, to signify *brave*. They
may be bought in Wales, in any quantities.

Letter, 1810

I have been today to an exhibition of Scotch portraits. High cheek bones are not favourable to the fine arts.

Letter, 1827

Pray tell me the sort of person you employ for cleaning the [Westminster Abbey] monuments. Is it a curate or a statuary, or is it a mere mason's labourer? Or does it (as in the case of a Scotchman caught and washed for the first time) require acid?

Letter, 1838

When shall I see Scotland again? Never shall I forget the happy days passed there, amidst odious smells, barbarous sounds, bad suppers, excellent hearts, and most enlightened and cultivated understandings.

Memoir

The Edinburgh Review

I proposed that we should set up a Review, and I remained long enough in Edinburgh to edit the first number. The motto I proposed for the Review was *Tenui musam meditamur avena* – 'We cultivate literature on a little oatmeal'. But this was too near the truth to be admitted.

Memoir

[We] intend to undertake a Review ... The rocks and shoals to be avoided are religion, politics, excessive severity, and irritable Scotchmen. If nothing else, the common sense of every man concerned will of course teach him the necessity of the utmost decency upon the two first points; in the third point I do not think we shall offend overmuch; and in the last the danger of a broken head will make us wise.

Letter, 1802

If any of [your friends] have a mind to barbecue a poet or two or strangle a metaphysician or do any other act of cruelty to the dull men of the earth we hope they will make our journal the receptacle of their exploits. We shall make it a point of honour neither to mutilate contributions, nor to reveal the names of contributors.

Letter, 1802

Campbell: 'Much of the Scotch marmalade is made in London.'
Smith: 'And much of the Edinburgh Review, too, let me tell you.'

I certainly, my dear Jeffrey ... do protest against your increasing and unprofitable scepticism. I exhort you to restrain the violent tendency of your nature for analysis, and to cultivate synthetical propensities. What's the use of virtue? What's the use of wealth? What's the use of honour? What's a guinea but a damned yellow circle? What's a chamber-pot but an infernal hollow sphere? The whole effort of your mind is to destroy. Because others build slightly and eagerly, you employ yourself in kicking down their houses, and contract a sort of aversion for the more honourable, useful and difficult task of building well yourself.

Letter, 1804

If you [my dear Jeffrey,] could be alarmed into the semblance of modesty, you would charm everybody; but remember my joke against you about the Moon and the Solar System – 'Damn the solar system! bad light – planets too distant – pestered with comets – feeble contrivance: could make a better with great ease!'

Letter, 1807

Brougham's review is not in good taste; he should have put on an air of serious concern, not raillery and ridicule; things are too serious for that. But it is very able. It is long yet vigorous, like the penis of a jackass.

Letter, 1809

Though I think it useful and creditable to attack what ought to be attacked, and expedient to use such weapons in attack as God has given us – gravity or gaiety, sense or sarcasm – yet there is moderation to be used in the frequency of attacks, and in the bitterness of attacks: and in both these points I believe I have sinned.

Letter, 1824

Literature

Words are an amazing barrier to the reception of truth.
Sketches of Moral Philosophy

Some men have only one book in them; others, a library.
Memoir

Brevity is in writing what charity is to all other virtues.
Righteousness is worth nothing without the one, nor
authorship without the other.
Edinburgh Review, 1809

As a general rule, run your pen through every other
word you have written; you have no idea what vigour it
will give your style.
Memoir

Whoever has had the great fortune to see Dr Parr's wig
must have observed that while it trespasses a little on
the orthodox magnitude of perukes in the anterior parts,
it scorns even episcopal limits behind, and swells out
into boundless convexity of frizz, the [great marvel] of
barbers, and the terror of the literary world. After the
manner of his wig, the Doctor has constructed his
sermon, giving us a discourse of no common length, and
subjoining an immeasurable mass of notes, which
appear to concern every learned thing, every learned
man, and almost every unlearned man since the
beginning of the world.
Edinburgh Review, 1802

Oh, don't read those twelve volumes until they are
made into a *consommé* of two.
Memoir

It is no more necessary that a man should remember the different dinners and suppers which have made him healthy, than the different books which have made him wise. Let us see the result of good food in a strong body, and the result of great reading in a full and powerful mind. *Sketches of Moral Philosophy*

Whatever you are from nature, keep to it; never desert your own line of talent. If Providence only intended you to write poses for rings or mottoes for twelfth-cakes, keep to poses and mottoes: a good motto for a twelfth-cake is more respectable than a villainous poem in twelve books. Be what nature intended you for, and you will succeed: be anything else, and you will be ten thousand times worse than nothing.
Sketches of Moral Philosophy

There is nothing of which Nature has been more bountiful than poets. They swarm like the spawn of cod-fish, with a vicious fecundity that invites and requires destruction. To publish verses is become a sort of evidence that a man wants sense; which is repelled not by writing good verses, but by writing excellent verses. *Edinburgh Review*, 1813

The main question as to a novel is, did it amuse? were you surprised at dinner coming so soon? did you mistake eleven for ten, and twelve for eleven? were you too late to dress? and did you sit up beyond the usual hour? If a novel produces these effects, it is good; if it does not – story, language, love, scandal itself cannot save it. It is only meant to please; and it must do that, or it does nothing. *Edinburgh Review*, 1826

Literature the Americans have none – no native literature, we mean. It is all imported.
Edinburgh Review, 1818

The Americans are a brave, industrious, and acute people: but they have hitherto given no indications of genius, and made no approaches to the heroic, either in their morality or character ... In the four quarters of the globe, who reads an American book? or goes to an American play ... ?   *Edinburgh Review*, 1820

Literature gives women a real and proper weight in society, but then they must use it with discretion; if the stocking is *blue*, the petticoat must be *long* ... the want of this has furnished food for ridicule in all ages.
                                                                        Memoir

Peregrine Courtenay: 'I always write best with an
    amanuensis.'
Smith: 'Oh, but are you quite sure he puts down what
    you dictate?'   *Memoir*

No furniture so charming as books, even if you never open them, or read a single word.   *Memoir*

Wrangham's library has overflowed all the lower rooms, and has crawled up the staircase, and covers the walls like an erysipelas.

I never read a book before reviewing it; it prejudices a man so.

Wit & Humour

Lightning must, I think, be the wit of heaven.

Memoir

It is imagined that wit is a sort of inexplicable visitation, that it comes and goes with the rapidity of lightning, and that it is quite as unattainable as beauty or just proportion. I am so much of the contrary way of thinking that I am convinced a man might sit down as systematically, and as successfully, to the study of wit, as he might to the study of mathematics: and I would answer for it that, by giving up only six hours a day to being witty, he should come on prodigiously before midsummer, so that his friends should hardly know him again.

Sketches of Moral Philosophy

The idea of utility is always inimical to the idea of wit.

Edinburgh Review

I have very little to say about puns; they are in very bad repute, and so they *ought* to be. The wit of language is so miserably inferior to the wit of ideas that it is very deservedly driven out of good company.

Sketches of Moral Philosophy

A true sarcasm is like a sword-stick – it appears, at first sight, to be much more innocent than it really is, till, all of a sudden, there leaps something out of it – sharp, deadly and incisive – which makes you tremble and recoil.

Sketches of Moral Philosophy

Professed wits, though they are generally courted for the
amusement they afford, are seldom respected for the
qualities they possess.

Sketches of Moral Philosophy

I mean to make some maxims, like Rochefoucauld, to
collect them by degrees out of my own head, and to
preserve them. My first is this: After having lived half
their lives respectably, many men get tired of honesty,
and many women of chastity.

Letter, 1808

You call me in your speech 'my facetious friend', and I
hasten to denominate you 'my solemn friend'; but you
and I must not run into common-place errors; you must
not think me necessarily foolish because I am facetious,
nor will I consider you necessarily wise because you are
grave.

Letter to Bishop Blomfield, 1840

Gastronomica

[Luttrell's] idea of heaven is eating *pâté de foie* to the sound of trumpets.

Bell, 198-9

I dined with the King at Brussels, eating Pâté de foie gras while the trumpets were sounding.

Letter, 1837

Recipe for a Salad

To make this condiment your poet begs,
The pounded yellow of two hard-boiled eggs;
Two boiled potatoes, passed through kitchen sieve,
Smoothness and softness to the salad give.
Let onion atoms lurk within the bowl,
And, half-suspected, animate the whole.
Of mordant mustard add a single spoon,
Distrust the condiment that bites so soon;
But deem it not, thou man of herbs, a fault
To add a double quantity of salt;
Four times the spoon with oil of Lucca crown,
And twice with vinegar procured from town;
And lastly o'er the flavoured compound toss
A magic soupçon of anchovy sauce.
Oh green and glorious! Oh, herbaceous treat!
'Twould tempt a dying anchorite to eat;
Back to the world he'd turn his fleeting soul,
And plunge his fingers in the salad-bowl!
Serenely full, the epicure would say,
'Fate cannot harm me, I have dined today.'

Bell, 101-2

It is admirable of you to send game to the clergy; that's what I call real piety; it reminds one of the primitive Christians.

Our hams here are the only true Hams; yours are only Shems and Japhets.   *Memoir*

If man had been only two feet high, he could not possibly have subdued the earth, and roasted and boiled animated nature in the way he now does.
                                Sketches of Moral Philosophy

Man wants but little here below,
As beef, veal, mutton, pork, lamb, venison show.
                                                        Memoir

I never yet knew the man who said he had ate enough asparagus.

How should herrings be dressed – or should they be eaten naked?

What is the use of fish or venison, when the backbone is 6 degrees below the freezing-point? Of all miserable habitations an English house in very hot or very cold weather is the worst.
                                                    Letter, 1819

What two ideas are more inseparable than Beer and Britannia? What event more awfully important to an English colony than the erection of its first brewhouse?
                                        Edinburgh Review, 1823

What use of wealth so luxurious and delightful as to light your house with gas? What folly, to have a diamond necklace or a Correggio, and not to light your house with gas! The splendour and glory of Lambton Hall make all other houses mean. How pitiful to submit to a farthing-candle existence, when science puts such gratification within your reach! Better to eat dry bread by the splendour of gas than to dine on wild beef with wax candles.

Letter, 1820

I heard a lady who sat next me, in a low, sweet voice, say, 'No gravy, Sir.' I had never seen her before, but I turned suddenly round and said, 'Madam, I have been looking for a person who disliked gravy all my life; let us swear eternal friendship.'

Memoir

Such is the horror the French have of our *cuisine*, that at a dinner given in honour of Guizot at the Athenaeum, they say his cook was heard to exclaim, 'Ah, mon pauvre maître! je ne le reverrai plus.'

Memoir

Do not imagine I am going to rat. I am a thoroughly honest, and I will say liberal, person, but have never given way to that puritanical feeling of the Whigs against dining with Tories:

    Tory and Whig in turn shall be my host,
    I taste no politics in boiled and roast.

Letter, 1834

I will fight you to the last drop of my ink, dine with you to the last drop of your claret, and entertain for you, *bibendo et scribendo*, sincere affection and respect.

Letter, 1837

They have lost that highest of human accomplishments,
the habit of giving dinners – an art which I am sure (for
the benefit of your friends) you will continue to excel in:
    Talk not of those who in the senate shine
    Give me the man with whom the jovial dine
    And break the ling'ring day with wit and wine.

Letter, 1834

I agree in the common praise of French living. Light
wines, and meat thoroughly subdued by human skill,
are more agreeable to me than the barbarous
Stone-Henge masses of meat with which we feed
ourselves.

Letter, 1835

Their delightful oil and their pleasant vinegar – *almost*
wine, like a lady who has *just* lost her character. Not the
liquid tallow and cut-throat acidity with which salads
are made in England.

Letter, 1835

I am convinced digestion is the great secret of life; and
that character, talents, virtues, and qualities are
powerfully affected by beef, mutton, pie-crust, and rich
soups. I have often thought that I could feed or starve
men into many virtues and vices, and affect them more
powerfully with my instruments of cookery than
Timotheus could do formerly with his lyre.

Letter, 1837

If there is a pure and elevated pleasure in this word, it is
a roast pheasant with bread sauce. Barn-door fowls for
dissenters, but for the real Churchman, the thirty-nine-
times articled clerk – the pheasant, the pheasant.

Letter, 1841

I have a breakfast of philosophers tomorrow at ten
punctually. Muffins and metaphysics, crumpets and
contradiction. Will you come?

Letter, 1841

Physician: 'I advise you to take a walk on an empty
  stomach.'
Smith: 'Whose?'

One of the greatest evils of old age is the advance of the
stomach over the rest of the body. It looks like the
accumulation of thousands of dinners and luncheons. It
looks like a pregnant woman in a cloth waistcoat, and as
if I were near my time and might reasonably look for
twins. I am very glad, my dear York, that Toasted
Cheese is brought in now after dinner. I have done with
fashions and look for realities.

Letter, 1840

I am making good progress – in fact, I am in a regular
train of promotion. From gruel, vermicelli, and sago, I
was promoted to panada, from thence to minced meat,
and (such is the effect of good conduct) I was elevated to
a mutton-chop. If you hear any tidings of 16 or 18 lbs of
human flesh, they belong to me – I look as if a curate
had been taken out of me.

Letter, 1844

Friends & Contemporaries

I have been reading Arnold's *Life*, by Stanley. Arnold
seems to have been a very pious, honest, learned, and
original man, without five grains of common sense. He
divided mankind into two parts – Dr Arnold, and *other
people*: with the former part remained all the sense,
philosophy, wisdom, and liberality.

Letter, 1844

Our friend ['Poodle' Byng] makes all the country smell
like Piccadilly.   *Memoir*

Read Boz's *Sketches* if you have not already read them. I
think them written with great power and that the soul of
Hogarth has migrated into the body of Dickens. I had
long heard of them but was deterred by the vulgarity of
the name.   Letter, 1837

Pray tell Dickens from me to remember that he is still
but a man – and that, however elated by this American
Deification, he must return to his Anthropic state, and
that he will find us (you and me) good friends but bad
idolaters.

Letter, 1842

I accept your obliging invitation conditionally. If I am
invited by any man of greater genius than yourself, or
one by whose works I have been more completely
interested, I will repudiate you, and dine with the more
splendid phenomenon of the two.

Letter to Dickens, 1842

[Of Thomas Grenville:] There, that is the man from
whom we all ought to learn how to grow old!

Memoir

[Lord Grey] – a fine nature, a just and vigorous
understanding, a sensitive disposition, and infirm
health. These are his leading traits. His excellencies are
courage, discretion, and practical sense; his deficiency, a
want of executive coarseness.   Letter, 1810

I have heard from Mrs Grote, who is very well, and
amusing herself with Horticulture and Democracy – the
most approved methods of growing cabbages and
destroying kings.   Letter, 1840

[To Mrs Grote:] Go where you will, do what you please.
I have the most perfect confidence in your *in*discretion.

'I think I may assert without fear of contradiction … '
Smith: 'Stop, sir, are you acquainted with Mr Hallam?'

I shall not be easy till [Jeffrey] is fairly on the Bench. His
robes, God knows, will cost him little; one buck rabbit
will clothe him to the heels.   Letter, 1829

Jeffrey is a man of rare talent and unbending integrity,
who has been honest in Scotland, which is as if he were
temperate and active at Capua.   Letter, 1829

[Luttrell] had not his usual soup-and-pattie look; there
was a forced smile upon his countenance which seemed
to indicate plain roast and boiled, and a sort of
apple-pudding depression as if he had been staying with
a clergyman.   Letter, 1829

Mr Luttrell is going gently down-hill, trusting that the cookery in another planet may be at least as good as this; but not without apprehension that for misconduct here he may be sentenced to a thousand years of tough mutton, or condemned to a little eternity of family dinners.   Letter, 1842

There is no limit to Macaulay's knowledge, on small subjects as well as great – he is like a book in breeches.
                                                                                          Memoir

Literature is [Macaulay's] vocation. Nothing would do him more good than a course of the Waters of Lethe; if he could forget half of what he reads he would be less suffocating than he is.   Letter, 1841

[Macaulay's] enemies might perhaps have said before (though I never did so) that he talked rather too much; but now he has occasional flashes of silence, that make his conversation perfectly delightful.   *Memoir*

[Tommy Moore] has one or two notes and looks when he is singing like a superannuated Cherubim.
                                                                                    Letter, 1843

When Prescott comes to England, a Caspian Sea of soup awaits him.   *Memoir*

Daniel Webster struck me much like a steam-engine in trousers.   *Memoir*

[The Dean of York] deserves to be preached to death by wild curates.   *Memoir*

[Samuel Rogers] has produced a couplet. When our friend is delivered of a couplet, with infinite labour and pain, he takes to his bed, has straw laid down, the knocker tied up, expects his friends to call and make inquiries, and the answer at the door inevitably is, 'Mr [Rogers] and his little couplet are as well as can be expected.' When he produces an Alexandrine he keeps his bed a day longer.

Memoir

There is not a better man in England than Lord John Russell; but his worst failure is that he is utterly ignorant of all moral fear; there is nothing he would not undertake. I believe he would perform the operation for the stone – build St Peter's – or assume (with or without ten minutes' notice) the command of the Channel fleet; and no one would discover by his manner that the patient had died – the Church tumbled down – and the Channel fleet been knocked to atoms.

Singleton Letters, II

You say, [Lord John,] you are not convinced by my pamphlet. I am afraid that I am a very arrogant person. But I do assure you that, in the fondest moments of self-conceit, the idea of convincing a Russell that he was wrong never crossed my mind.

Letter, 1837

I hope you have read [Dugald] Stewart's book, and are far gone in the philosophy of mind, a science as he repeatedly tells us still in its infancy: I propose myself to wait till it comes to years of discretion.

Letter, 1810

Science is his forte, and omniscience his foible. [Of William Whewell, Master of Trinity College, Cambridge.]

Town & Country

I believe the parallelogram between Oxford-street, Piccadilly, Regent-street, and Hyde Park encloses more intelligence and human ability, to say nothing of wealth and beauty, than the world has ever collected in such a space before.

Memoir

A few yards in London dissolve or cement friendship.

Brighton Pavilion looks as if St Paul's had slipped down to Brighton and pupped.

I am better in health avoiding all fermented liquors, and drinking nothing but London water with a million of insects in every drop; he who drinks a tumbler of London water has literally in his stomach more animated beings than there are men, women and children on the face of the globe.

Letter, 1834

A joke goes a great way in the country. I have known one last pretty well for seven years.

Memoir

I have brought all my children up to town. It is the first time they have ever seen four people together, except on remarkably fine days at the parish churches.

Letter, 1818

Our neighbours here are in the common line – port and
sherry for dinner, hail, rain and snow for conversation;
but the best people in any place come slowly to light and
lie, like macaroon cakes at the bottom of an Italian
Cream, last and best.

Letter, 1829

The neighbourhood much the same as all other
neighbourhoods. Red wine and white, soup and fish,
bad wit and good nature.

Letter, 1929

The summer and the country have no charms for me. I
look forward anxiously to the return of bad weather,
coal fires, and good society in a crowded city. I have no
relish for the country; it is a kind of healthy grave. I am
afraid you are not exempt from the delusions of flowers,
green turf, and birds; they all afford slight gratification,
but not worth an hour of rational conversation: and
rational conversation in sufficient quantities is only to be
had from the congregation of a million people in one
spot.

Letter, 1838

The country is most dreadful! The real use of it is to find
food for cities; but as for a residence of any man who is
neither butcher nor baker, nor food-grower in any of its
branches, it is a dreadful waste of existence and abuse of
life.

Letter, 1841

Church & Clergy

Don't you know, as the French say, there are three sexes
– men, women, and clergymen.   *Memoir*

The clergy of England have no more influence over the
people at large than the cheesemongers of England.
                                                  Memoir

Preaching has become a bye-word for long and dull
conversation of any kind; and whoever wishes to imply,
in any piece of writing, the absence of every thing
agreeable and inviting, calls it a sermon.
                                                  Memoir

The great object of modern sermons is to hazard
nothing: their characteristic is decent debility, which
alike guards their authors from ludicrous errors, and
precludes them from striking beauties.
                                   Edinburgh Review, 1802

A sparrow fluttering about the church is an antagonist
which the most profound theologian in Europe is wholly
unable to overcome.   *Memoir*

I am convinced we should do no great injury to the
cause of religion if we remembered the old combination
of *arae et foci*, and kept our churches a little warmer. An
experienced clergyman can pretty well estimate the
number of his audience by the indications of a sensible
thermometer.   *Memoir*

The [Dissenters'] Tabernacle really is to the church what
Sadler's Wells is to the drama.

Edinburgh Review, 1808

The English, generally remarkable for doing very good
things in a very bad manner, seem to have reserved the
maturity and the plenitude of their awkwardness for the
pulpit. A clergyman clings to his velvet cushion with
either hand, keeps his eye riveted upon his book, speaks
of the ecstasies of joy and fear with a voice and a face
which indicate neither, and pinions his body and soul
into the same attitude of limb and thought, for fear of
being called theatrical and affected ... Is it wonder, then,
that every semi-delirious sectary who pours forth his
animated nonsense with the genuine look and voice of
passion, should gesticulate away the congregation of the
most profound and learned divine of the Established
Church, and in two Sundays preach him bare to the very
sexton?

Memoir

Bishops are men; not always the wisest of men; not
always preferred for eminent virtues and talents, or for
any good reason whatever known to the public. They
are almost always devoid of striking and indecorous
vices; but a man may be very shallow, very arrogant,
and very vindictive, though a bishop; and pursue with
unrelenting hatred a subordinate clergyman, whose
principles he dislikes and whose genius he fears.

Edinburgh Review, 1809

What bishops like best in their clergy is a dropping-
down-deadness of manner.

Singleton Letters, I

How can a bishop marry? How can he flirt? The most he
can say is, 'I will see you in the vestry after service'.

Memoir

I have seen in the course of my life, as the mind of the prelate decayed, wife bishops, daughter bishops, butler bishops, and even cook and housekeeper bishops.

Edinburgh Review, 1809

Archbishop: 'I hear, Mr Smith, you do not approve of much riding for the clergy.'
Smith: 'Why, my Lord, perhaps there is not *much objection*, provided they do not ride too well, and stick out their toes professionally.' *Memoir*

If anything ever endangers the Church, it will be the strong propensity to shooting for which the clergy are remarkable. Ten thousand good shots dispersed over the country do more harm to the cause of religion than the arguments of Voltaire and Rousseau.

Letter, 1809

Did you say 'a Quaker baby'? Impossible! there is no such thing; there never was; they are always born broad-brimmed and in full quake.

Memoir

Why are you an honest man? You might have been Bishop of London. Will no time and no example cure you? Repent and do not go unmitred to your tomb.

Letter, 1813

The Bishop appears to be in a fog, and as daylight breaks in upon him he will be rather disposed to disown his panic. The noise he hears is not roaring, but braying; the teeth and the mane are all imaginary; there is nothing but ears. It is not a lion that stops the way, but an ass.

Edinburgh Review, 1813

Men of small incomes have often very acute feelings; and a Curate trod on feels a pang as great as when a Bishop is refuted.

Edinburgh Review, 1822

His Lordship boasts that he has excluded only two curates. So the Emperor of Hayti boasted that he had only cut off two persons' heads for disagreeable behaviour at his table.

Edinburgh Review, 1822

The longer we live, the more we are convinced of the justice of the old saying, that 'an ounce of mother wit is worth a pound of clergy'; that discretion, gentle manners, common sense, and good nature are, in men of high ecclesiastical station, of far greater importance than the greatest skill in discriminating between sublapsarian and supralapsarian doctrines.

Edinburgh Review, 1822

The campanero may be heard three miles! – this single little bird being more powerful than the belfry of a cathedral, ringing for a new dean – just appointed on account of shabby politics, small understanding, and good family!

Edinburgh Review, 1826

[The sloth] moves suspended, rests suspended, sleeps suspended, and passes his life in suspense – like a young clergyman distantly related to a bishop.

Edinburgh Review, 1826

The Archbishop has sprained the *tendo Athanasii*, which in laymen is the *tendo Achillis*.

How very much the great emoluments of the Church are flung open to the lowest ranks of the community. Butchers, bakers, publicans, schoolmasters, are perpetually seeing their children elevated to the mitre ... Young Crumpet is sent to school – takes to his books – spends the best years of his life, as all eminent Englishmen do, in making Latin verses – knows that the *crum* in crum-pet is long, and the *pet* short – goes to the University – gets a prize for an Essay on the Dispersion of the Jews – takes orders – becomes a Bishop's chaplain – has a young nobleman for his pupil – publishes an useless classic, and a serious call to the unconverted – and then goes through the Elysian transitions of Prebendary, Dean, Prelate, and the long train of purple, profit, and power.

Singleton Letters, II

Is it necessary that the Archbishop of Canterbury should give feasts to aristocratic London; and that the domestics of the prelacy should stand with swords and bag-wigs round pig, and turkey, and venison, to defend, as it were, the Orthodox gastronome from the fierce Unitarian, the fell Baptist, and all the famished children of Dissent?

Singleton Letters, II

I met some Navy chaplains – the Church navigant.

The Bishop of Gloucester ... says that I have not been appointed to my situation as Canon of St Paul's for my piety and learning, but because I am a scoffer and a jester. Is not this rather strong for a Bishop, and does it not appear to you, Mr Archdeacon, as rather too close an imitation of that language which is used in the apostolic occupation of trafficking in fish?

Singleton Letters, III

Walking with the Bishop of Exeter by a shop on which was written up 'Tongues cured here': 'Shall we go in, my lord?'

I must believe in the Apostolic succession, there being no other way of accounting for the descent of the Bishop of Exeter from Judas Iscariot.

The advice I sent to the Bishop of New Zealand, when he had to receive the cannibal chiefs there, was to say to them: 'I deeply regret, Sirs, to have nothing on my own table suited to your tastes, but you will find plenty of cold curate and roasted clergyman on the sideboard.'

Memoir

To a lady: 'If you'll sing, I'll preach.'

'Why are you stroking the shell?', said my father. 'Oh, to please the turtle.' 'Why, child, you might as well stroke the dome of St Paul's, to please the Dean and Chapter.'

Memoir

To go to St Paul's is certain death. The thermometer is several degrees below zero. My sentences are frozen as they come out of my mouth, and are thawed in the course of summer, making strange noises and unexpected assertions in various parts of the church.

Letter, November 1833

What is real piety? What is true attachment to the Church? How are these fine feelings best evinced? The answer is plain: by sending strawberries to a clergyman. Many thanks.

Letter, 1834

What a pleasing reflection is that of the Archbishops dwelling together – what an accumulation of power, what a luxury of sanctity, the Right Revd Pelion on the Right Revd Ossa, Gog and Magog. What a Halo of Holiness must surround them.

Letter, 1835

Do not flatter yourself with the delusive hope of a slumber; I preach violently, and there is a strong smell of sulphur in my sermons.

Letter, 1839

The Virgers [of St Paul's] have the strictest orders not to accept money, just as the footmen have in all serious families not to kiss the maids. That these orders are equally well obeyed neither you nor I have the smallest doubt.

Letter, 1839

You are a romantic canon to talk about warming St Paul's. The only real way of doing it is to warm the County of Middlesex, to which our revenues are hardly adequate.

Letter, 1840

I have seen nobody, since I saw you, but persons in orders. My only varieties are vicars, rectors, curates, and every now and then (by way of turbot) an archdeacon.

Letter, 1843

Sydney Smith feeling so ill and confused that he could not remember whether there were nine Articles and thirty-nine Muses, or the contrary.

Monckton Milnes

We naturally lose illusions as we get older, like teeth, but there is no Cartwright to fit a new set into our understandings. I have, alas! only one illusion left, and that is the Archbishop of Canterbury [Howley].

Memoir

Politics

It is always considered a piece of impertinence in England if a man of less than two or three thousand a year has any opinions at all on important subjects.

Preface to *Collected Works*

I believe the English are the most disagreeable people under the sun; not so much because Mr John Bull disdains to talk, as that the respected individual has nothing to say, and because he totally neglects manners.

Memoir

I have a boundless confidence in the English character; I believe that they have more real religion, more probity, more knowledge, and more genuine worth, than exists in the whole world besides.

Sketches of Moral Philosophy

If I could see good measures pursued, I care not a farthing who is in power; but I have a passionate love for common justice, and for common sense, and I abhor and despise every man who builds up his political fortune upon their ruin.

Plymley's Letters, I

The moment the very name of Ireland is mentioned, the English seem to bid adieu to common feeling, common prudence, and common sense, and to act with the barbarity of tyrants, and the fatuity of idiots.

Plymley's Letters, II

When I hear any man talk of an unalterable law, the only
effect it has upon me is to convince me that he is an
unalterable fool.   *Plymley's Letters*, IV

Our conduct to Ireland, during the whole of this war,
has been that of a man who subscribes to hospitals,
weeps at charity sermons, carries out broth and blankets
to beggars, and then comes home and beats his wife and
children.   *Plymley's Letters*, IV

Ireland a millstone about your neck! Why is it not a
stone of Ajax in your hand?   *Plymley's Letters*, VI

To talk of not acting from fear is mere parliamentary
cant. From what motive but fear, I should be glad to
know, have all the improvements in our constitution
proceeded? I question if any justice has ever been done
to large masses of mankind from any other motive.
                                         Plymley's Letters, VI

[The Foreign Secretary] is a fly in amber, nobody cares
about the fly; the only question is, How the devil did it
get there? Nor did I attack him for the love of glory, but
from the love of utility, as a burgomaster hunts a rat in a
Dutch dyke, for fear it should flood a province.
                                         Plymley's Letters, VII

I detest that state of society which extends unequal
degrees of protection to different creeds and
persuasions; and I cannot describe to you the contempt I
feel for a man who, calling himself a statesman, defends
a system which fills the heart of every Irishman with
treason, and makes his allegiance prudence, not choice.
                                         Plymley's Letters, IX

If I lived at Hampstead [like Spencer Perceval] upon stewed meats and claret; if I walked to church every Sunday before eleven young gentlemen of my own begetting, with their faces washed, and their hair pleasingly combed: if the Almighty had blessed me with every earthly comfort – how awfully would I pause before I sent forth the flame and the sword over the cabins of the poor, brave, generous, open-hearted peasants of Ireland!

Plymley's Letters, IX

Loyalty, within the bounds of reason and moderation, is one of the great instruments of English happiness; but the love of the King may easily become more strong than the love of the kingdom, and we may lose sight of the public welfare in our exaggerated admiration of him who is appointed to reign only for its promotion and support. *Plymley's Letters*, X

The only foundation of political liberty is the spirit of the people: and the only circumstance which makes a lively impression upon their senses, and powerfully reminds them of their importance, their power, and their rights, is the periodical choice of their representatives.

Edinburgh Review, 1803

A nation grown free in a single day is a child born with the limbs and the vigour of a man, who would take a drawn sword for his rattle, and set the house in a blaze, that he might chuckle over the splendour.

Edinburgh Review, 1803

The prize of supreme power is too tempting to admit of fair play in the game of ambition; and it is wise to lessen its value by dividing it.

Edinburgh Review, 1803

The partial creation of peers for life only, would appear
to remedy a very material defect in the English
constitution ... The most useless and offensive tumour
in the body politic is the titled son of a great man whose
merit has placed him in the peerage. The name, face, and
perhaps the pension, remain. The daemon is gone: or
there is a slight flavour from the cask, but it is empty.
Edinburgh Review, 1803

I now consider the war between France and England no
longer as an occasional quarrel or temporary dispute,
but as an antipathy and national horror, after the same
kind as subsists between the kite and the crow, or the
churchwarden and the pauper, the weasel and the rat,
the parson and the Deist, the bailiff and the half-pay
Captain, etc., who have persecuted each other from the
beginning of time, and will peck, swear, fly, preach at,
and lie in wait for each other till the end of time.
Memoir

All establishments die of dignity. They are too proud to
think themselves ill, and to take a little physic.
Edinburgh Review, 1811

My astonishment was very great at reading Canning's
challenge to the anonymous pamphleteer ... What
sympathy can a wit by profession, a provoker and
discoverer of other men's weaknesses, expect for his
literary woes? What does a politician know of his trade,
when twenty years have not made him pamphlet-proof?
Letter, 1818

So great and so long has been the misgovernment of
Ireland, that we verily believe the empire would be
much stronger if every thing was open sea between the
England and the Atlantic, and if skates and cod-fish
swam over the fair land of Ulster.
Edinburgh Review, 1820

The follies of one century are scarcely credible in that which succeeds it. A grandmama of 1827 is as wise as a very wise man of 1727. If the world lasts till 1927, the grandmamas of that period will be far wiser than the tiptop No Popery men of this day. That this childish nonsense will have got out of the drawing-room, there can be no doubt.

Edinburgh Review, 1827

All great alterations in human affairs are produced by compromise.

Edinburgh Review, 1827

The world never yet saw so extravagant a government as the Government of England. Not only is economy not practised – but it is despised ... Such a scene of extravagance, corruption, and expense as must paralyse the industry, and mar the fortunes, of the most industrious, spirited people that ever existed.

Edinburgh Review, 1827

The new Beer Bill has begun its operations. Everybody is drunk. Those who are not singing are sprawling. The sovereign people are in a beastly state.

Letter, 1830

There is only one principle of public conduct – Do what you think right, and take place and power as an accident. Upon any other plan, office is shabbiness, labour, and sorrow.

Taunton Speech, 1831

The majority of the new Members will be landed gentlemen: their genus is utterly distinct from the revolutionary tribe; they have molar teeth; they are destitute of the carnivorous and incisive jaws of political adventurers. There will be mistakes at first, as there are in all changes. All young ladies will imagine (as soon as this Bill is carried) that they will be instantly married. Schoolboys believe that gerunds and supines will be abolished, and that currant tarts must ultimately come down in price; the corporal and sergeant are sure of double pay; bad poets will expect a demand for their epics. Fools will be disappointed, as they always are; reasonable men, who know what to expect, will find that a very serious good has been obtained.

Reform Speech, 1831

At [Edinburgh] we are told, by Mr Dundas, that there is no eagerness for Reform. Five minutes before Moses struck the rock, this gentleman would have said that there was no eagerness for water.   Reform Speech, 1831

The attempt of the Lords to stop the progress of Reform reminds me very forcibly of the great storm of Sidmouth, and of the conduct of the excellent Mrs Partington on that occasion. In the winter of 1824 there set in a great flood upon that town – the tide rose to an incredible height, the waves rushed in upon the houses, and everything was threatened with destruction! In the midst of this sublime and terrible storm, Dame Partington, who lived upon the beach, was seen at the door of her house with mop and pattens, trundling her mop, squeezing out the sea-water, and vigorously pushing away the Atlantic Ocean. The Atlantic was roused. Mrs Partington's spirit was up; but I need not tell you that the contest was unequal. The Atlantic Ocean beat Mrs Partington. She was excellent at a slop, or a puddle, but she should not have meddled with a tempest. Gentlemen, be at your ease – be quiet and steady. You will beat Mrs Partington.

Taunton Speech on Parliamentary Reform, 1831

All gradation and caution have been banished since the Reform Bill; rapid high-pressure wisdom is the only agent in public affairs.

Singleton Letters, II

No man, I fear, can effect great benefits for his country without some sacrifice of the minor virtues.

The plough is not a political machine: the loom and the steam-engine are furiously political, but the plough is not.   *Letter on the Ballot*

Ballot is a mere illusion, but universal suffrage is not an illusion. The common people will get nothing by the one, but they will gain everything, and *ruin* everything, by the last.

Letter on the Ballot

I am astonished that these Ministers neglect the common precaution of a foolometer, with which no public man should be unprovided: I mean the acquaintance and society of three or four regular British fools as a test of public opinion. Every Cabinet Minister should judge of all his measures by a foolometer, as a navigator crowds or shortens sail by the barometer in his cabin.

Singleton Letters, II

Sterling: 'If you Whigs send Campbell Chancellor to Ireland, you will drive them mad.'
Smith: 'And a very short stage to go, my lord, and no postilions to pay.'

The House of Commons, as a near relation of mine once observed, has more good taste than any man in it.

Letter, 1842

You must not forget of me that I began attacking abuses between 35 and 40 years ago when it was safer almost to be a felon than a reformer; and you must not mistake my afternoon nonsense for my serious, and morning, opinions.

Letter, 1835

Toleration & Intolerance

Human beings cling to their delicious tyrannies, and to their exquisite nonsense, like a drunkard to his bottle, and go on till death stares them in the face.

Letters on the Irish Clergy

A bigot delights in public ridicule, for he begins to think himself a martyr. *Plymley's Letters*, I

No eel in the well-sanded fist of a cook-maid, upon the eve of being skinned, ever twisted and writhed as an orthodox parson does when he is compelled by the gripe of reason to admit anything in favour of a Dissenter.

Plymley's Letters, II

There is no fantasy, however wild, that a man may not persuade himself that he cherishes from motives of conscience.

Plymley's Letters, IV

When a country squire hears of an ape, his first feeling is to give it nuts and apples; when he hears of a Dissenter, his immediate response is to commit it to the county jail, to shave its head, to alter its customary food, and to have it privately whipped.

Plymley's Letters, V

Toleration is a great good, and a good to be imitated, come from whom it will.

Plymley's Letters, VIII

If men are to be fools, I would rather they were fools in little matters than in great; dullness turned up with temerity is a livery all the worse for the facings; and the most tremendous of all things is the magnanimity of a dunce. *Plymley's Letters*, X

Toleration never had a present tense, nor taxation a future one.
Edinburgh Review, 1808

Religion is so noble and powerful a consideration, it is so buoyant and insubmergible, that it may be made, by fanatics, to carry with it any degree of error and of serious absurdity.
Edinburgh Review, 1808

If experience has taught us anything, it is the absurdity of controlling men's notions of eternity by acts of Parliament. *Edinburgh Review*, 1808

It is the easiest of all things, too, in this country, to make Englishmen believe that those who oppose the Government wish to ruin the country.
Edinburgh Review, 1809

Nothing dies so hard and rallies so often as intolerance.
Edinburgh Review, 1811

What right has any Government to dictate to any man who shall guide him to heaven, any more than it has to persecute the religious tenets by which he hopes to arrive there?
Edinburgh Review, 1811

The best way of answering a bad argument is not to stop it, but to let it go on its course till it leaps over the boundaries of common sense.

Edinburgh Review, 1821

I insisted [my curate] should come and vote against me. I assured him nothing would give me more pain than to think I had prevented, in any man, the free expression of honest opinions.

Speech on Catholic Emancipation, 1825

This week I publish a pamphlet on the Catholic question. What a detestable subject – stale, threadbare and exhausted – but ancient errors cannot be met with fresh refutations.

Letter, 1826

I hate the insolence, persecution and intolerance which so often pass under the name of religion … but I have an unaffected horror of irreligion and impiety, and every principle of suspicion and fear would be excited in me by a man who professed himself an Infidel.

Letter, 1827

You may as well attempt to poultice off the humps of a camel's back as to cure mankind of these little corruptions.

Singleton Letters, II

I rejoice in the temple which has been reared to Toleration; and I am proud that I worked as a bricklayer's labourer at it – without pay, and with the enmity and abuse of those who were unfavourable to its construction.

Letter [on Catholic Emancipation], 1830

Law & Punishment

Justice is pleasant, even when she destroys.

Sketches of Moral Philosophy

The only true way to make the mass of mankind see the beauty of justice is by showing them in pretty plain terms the consequences of injustice.

Plymley's Letters, VI

An English mob which, to a foreigner, might convey the belief of an impending massacre, is often contented by the demolition of a few windows.

Edinburgh Review, 1803

The true way to attack vice is by setting something else against it.

Edinburgh Review, 1810

Because punishment does not annihilate crime, it is folly to say it does not lessen it. It did not stop the murder of Mrs Donatty; but how many Mrs Donattys has it kept alive!

Edinburgh Review, 1824

Punishments are not merely to be estimated by pain to the limbs, but by the feelings of the mind.

Edinburgh Review, 1824

Mrs Fry is an amiable excellent woman, and ten thousand times better than the infamous neglect that preceded her; but hers is not the method to stop crimes ... There must be a great deal of solitude; coarse food; a dress of shame; hard, incessant, irksome, external labour; a planned and regulated and unrelenting exclusion of happiness and comfort.

Edinburgh Review, 1822

The Americans, we believe, are the first persons who have discarded the tailor in the administration of justice, and his auxiliary the barber – two persons of endless importance to the codes and pandects of Europe. A judge administers justice, without a calorific wig and parti-coloured gown, in a coat and pantaloons. He is obeyed, however: and life and property are not badly protected in the United States.

Edinburgh Review, 1824

There are, in every county in England, large public schools maintained at the expense of the county, for the encouragement of profligacy and vice, and for providing a proper succession of housebreakers, profligates, and thieves ... The moment any young person evinces the slightest propensity for these pursuits, he is provided with food, clothing and lodging, and put to his studies under the most accomplished thieves and cut-throats the county can supply.

Edinburgh Review [on Prisons], 1829

Education

Boys are as certainly spoilt who remain a long time at home as meat is corrupted by being kept in too close a larder.   Letter, 1813

The first year of Westminster in college is severe – an intense system of tyranny, of which the English are very fond, and think it fits a boy for the world; but the world, bad as it is, has nothing half so bad.

Letter, 1820

The *head* of a public school is generally a very conceited young man, utterly ignorant of his own dimensions, and losing all that habit of conciliation towards others, and that anxiety for self-improvement, which result from the natural modesty of youth. Nor is this conceit very easily and speedily got rid of; we have seen ... public-school importance lasting through the half of after-life, strutting in lawn, swelling in ermine, and displaying itself, both ridiculously and offensively, in the haunts and business of bearded men.

Edinburgh Review, 1810

Every young man must be exposed to temptation: he cannot learn the ways of men without being witness to their vices. If you attempt to preserve him from danger by keeping him out of the way of it, you render him quite unfit for any style of life in which he may be placed. The great point is, not to turn him out too soon, and to give him a pilot at first.

Sketches of Moral Philosophy

To almost every Englishman up to the age of three or four and twenty, classical learning has been the great object of existence; and no man is very apt to suspect, or very much pleased to hear, that what he has done for so long a time was not worth doing.

Edinburgh Review, 1809

It is the greatest and first use of history, to show us the sublime in morals, and to tell us what great men have done in perilous seasons. Such beings, and such actions, dignify our nature, and breathe into us a virtuous pride which is the parent of every good.

Sketches of Moral Philosophy

Education gives fecundity of thought, copiousness of illustration, quickness, vigour, fancy, words, images, and illustrations; it decorates every common thing, and gives the power of trifling without being undignified and absurd.

Edinburgh Review, 1810

—— has been to Cambridge to place his son; in other words, he has put him there to spend his money, to lose what good qualities he has, and to gain nothing useful in return. If men made no more progress in the common arts of life than they have in education, we should at the moment be dividing our food with our fingers, and drinking out of the palms of our hands.   Letter, 1831

When an University has been doing useless things for a long time, it appears at first degrading to them to be useful.

Edinburgh Review, 1809

There is one piece of advice, in a life of study, which I think no one will object to: that is, every now and then, to be completely idle, to do nothing at all.

Sketches of Moral Philosophy

Women & Marriage

There is a very general notion, that if you once suffer women to eat of the tree of knowledge, the rest of the family will very soon be reduced to the same kind of aerial and unsatisfactory diet.

Edinburgh Review, 1810

If you neglect to educate the mind of a woman, by the speculative difficulties which occur in literature, it can never be educated at all: if you do not effectually arouse it by education, it must remain forever languid. Uneducated men may escape intellectual degradation; uneducated women cannot.

Edinburgh Review, 1810

Diffuse knowledge generally among women, and you will at once cure the conceit which knowledge occasions when it is rare.

Edinburgh Review, 1810

[Marriage] resembles a pair of shears, so joined that they cannot be separated; often moving in opposite directions, yet always punishing any one who comes between them.

Memoir

By what curious links, and fantastical relations, are mankind connected together! At the distance of half the globe, a Hindoo gains his support by groping at the bottom of the sea for the morbid concretion of a shellfish, to decorate the throat of a London alderman's wife.

Edinburgh Review, 1803

Ah, you flavour everything; you are the vanille of society.

Memoir

Her smile is so radiant that I believe it would force even a gooseberry-bush into flower.

Memoir

Don't mind the caprices of fashionable women; they are as gross as poodles fed on milk and muffins.

Memoir

When so showy a woman as Mrs —— appears at a place, though there is no garrison within twelve miles, the horizon is immediately clouded with Majors.

Memoir

To say that I am sure I shall deserve the character you have given me would be as absurd as if a lady were to express an absolute certainty of her future virtue.

Letter, 1820

Counsels & Maxims

A great deal of talent is lost to the world for the want of a little courage. *Sketches of Moral Philosophy*

Mankind are always happy for having been happy; so that if you make them happy now, you make them happy twenty years hence by the memory of it. *Sketches of Moral Philosophy*

Avoid shame, but do not seek glory; nothing so expensive as glory. *Memoir*

All honest men, whether counts or cobblers, are of the same rank, if classed by moral distinctions. *Edinburgh Review, 1823*

Piety, stretched beyond a certain point, is the parent of impiety. *Memoir*

The man who places religion upon a false basis is the greatest enemy to religion. *Edinburgh Review, 1808*

You never expected justice from a company, did you? They have neither a soul to lose, nor a body to kick. *Memoir*

Among the smaller duties of life, I hardly know one more important than that of not praising where praise is not due. *Memoir*

Never gamble at the game of life; be content to play for sixpences; marriage is too high a stake for a wise man to risk. *Memoir*

There are many occasions in life where it is possible to effect by forgiveness every object which you propose to effect by resentment. *Sermon on Forgiveness*

If you desire the common people to treat you as a
gentleman, you must conduct yourself as a gentleman
should do to them.   *Memoir*

You find people ready enough to do the Samaritan,
without the oil and twopence.   *Memoir*

Death must be distinguished from dying, with which it
is often confounded.   *Memoir*

If you choose to present the various parts in life by holes
upon a table, of different shapes – some circular, some
triangular, some square, some oblong – and the persons
acting these by bits of wood of similar shapes, we shall
generally find that the triangular person has got into the
square hole, the oblong into the triangular, and the
square person has squeezed himself into the round hole.
The officer and the office, the doer and the thing done,
seldom fit so exactly that we can say they were almost
made for each other.

Sketches of Moral Philosophy

As I am an adviser by trade, allow me to recommend
moderation in pursuing the pleasures of the chase. The
fox was given to mankind not for business, but for
amusement.   *Letter, 1826*

What makes a fire so pleasant is that it is a live thing in a
dead room.   *Memoir*

I like in you very much that you are a religious woman,
because, though I have an infinite hatred and contempt
for the nonsense which often passes under, and
disgraces, the name of religion, I am very much pleased
when I see anybody religious for hope and comfort, not
for insolence and interest.   *Letter, 1819*

Everybody is haunted with spectres and apparitions of
sorrow, and the imaginary griefs of life are greater than
the real. Whatever the English zenith may be, the
horizon is almost always of a sombre colour.
                                                   Letter, 1819

Advice on Low Spirits

Nobody has suffered more from low spirits than I have done, so I feel for you. 1. Live as well and drink as much wine as you dare. 2. Go in to the shower-bath with a small quantity of water at a temperature low enough to give you a *slight* sensation of cold – 75 or 80°. 3. Amusing books. 4. Short views of human life not farther than dinner or tea. 5. Be as busy as you can. 6. See as much as you can of those friends who respect and like you; 7. and of those acquaintance who amuse you. 8. Make no secret of low spirits to your friends but talk of them fully: they are always the worse for dignified concealment. 9. Attend to the effects tea and coffee produce upon you. 10. Compare your lot with that of other people. 11. Don't expect too much of human life, a sorry business at best. 12. Avoid poetry, dramatic representations (except comedy), music, serious novels, melancholy sentimental people, and everything likely to excite feeling or emotion not ending in active benevolence. 13. Do good and endeavour to please everybody of every degree. 14. Be as much as you can in the open air without fatigue. 15. Make the room where you commonly sit gay and pleasant. 16. Struggle little by little against idleness. 17. Don't be too severe upon yourself, but do yourself justice. 18. Keep good, blazing fires. 19. Be firm and constant in the exercise of rational religion. 20. Believe me dear Lady Georgiana very truly yours, SYDNEY SMITH.

Letter, 1820